BROADWAY CLASSICS
FOR PIANO SOLO

ARRANGED BY MARK HAYES

ISBN 978-1-5400-2558-6

HAL•LEONARD®

Visit Hal Leonard Online at
www.halleonard.com

Contact us:
Hal Leonard
7777 West Bluemound Road
Milwaukee, WI 53213
Email: info@halleonard.com

In Europe, contact:
Hal Leonard Europe Limited
42 Wigmore Street
Marylebone, London, W1U 2RN
Email: info@halleonardeurope.com

In Australia, contact:
Hal Leonard Australia Pty. Ltd.
4 Lentara Court
Cheltenham, Victoria, 3192 Australia
Email: info@halleonard.com.au

ABOUT THE ARRANGER

MARK HAYES is an award-winning concert pianist, composer, arranger and conductor of international renown. His personal catalog totals over 1,500 published works of all kinds. Mark received a Bachelor of Music degree (summa cum laude) in Piano Performance from Baylor University in 1975. He has conducted the SWACDA & MCDA Community & Church Honor Choir and has served as a frequent guest conductor at Lincoln Center, the National Cathedral and Carnegie Hall, featuring works such as his *Te Deum, Magnificat, Gloria* and *International Carol Suites*.

In 2010, Baylor University Center for Christian Music Studies honored Mark with the Award for Exemplary Leadership in Christian Music. He conducted the world premiere of his *Requiem* at Lincoln Center in May 2013. In October 2014, Hayes conducted his *Requiem* at St. Ignatius Basilica in Rome, Italy as part of The Festival Pro Musica E Arte Sacra, sponsored by the Vatican. He was commissioned by St. Paul's Co-educational College in Hong Kong to write a work for treble voices, mixed voices and orchestra for their 100th anniversary and also conducted the world premiere in Hong Kong (December 2015).

Hayes wrote the musical score for *Civil War Voices*, which won six awards at the Midtown International Theatre Festival in New York City (July 2010). He orchestrated the hit musical *Madame Buttermilk* by Ross Carter and arranged the music for *We'll Meet Again*, a new musical by Jim Harris.

Mark's passion is writing for the piano. He has over 65 piano books in print, spanning a variety of styles such as Gospel, Classical, Jazz and Broadway. In addition to his involvement in the sacred and secular choral music fields, Hayes is an accomplished orchestrator and record producer. Whether concertizing on the other side of the globe or composing at his home in Kansas City, Missouri, Mark is blessed to live out his mission "to create beautiful music for the world."

4

ALL I ASK OF YOU
THE PHANTOM OF THE OPERA

8

BEAUTY AND THE BEAST
BEAUTY AND THE BEAST:
THE BROADWAY MUSICAL

11

CAN YOU FEEL THE LOVE TONIGHT
THE LION KING:
THE BROADWAY MUSICAL

16

CORNER OF THE SKY
PIPPIN

22

EVERYTHING'S COMING UP ROSES
GYPSY

28

I DREAMED A DREAM
LES MISÉRABLES

32

NOT WHILE I'M AROUND
SWEENEY TODD

36

SEASONS OF LOVE
RENT

40

SEND IN THE CLOWNS
A LITTLE NIGHT MUSIC

44

TILL THERE WAS YOU
THE MUSIC MAN

ALL I ASK OF YOU
from THE PHANTOM OF THE OPERA

Music by ANDREW LLOYD WEBBER
Lyrics by CHARLES HART
Additional Lyrics by RICHARD STILGOE
Arranged by Mark Hayes

BEAUTY AND THE BEAST

from BEAUTY AND THE BEAST: THE BROADWAY MUSICAL

Music by ALAN MENKEN
Lyrics by HOWARD ASHMAN
Arranged by Mark Hayes

Can You Feel The Love Tonight

from THE LION KING: THE BROADWAY MUSICAL

Music by ELTON JOHN
Words by TIM RICE
Arranged by Mark Hayes

CORNER OF THE SKY

from PIPPIN

Music and Lyrics by
STEPHEN SCHWARTZ
Arranged by Mark Hayes

EVERYTHING'S COMING UP ROSES

from GYPSY

Lyrics by STEPHEN SONDHEIM
Music by JULE STYNE
Arranged by Mark Hayes

Lively (= ca. 124)

I DREAMED A DREAM

from LES MISÉRABLES

Music by CLAUDE-MICHEL SCHÖNBERG
Lyrics by ALAIN BOUBLIL,
JEAN-MARC NATEL and HERBERT KRETZMER
Arranged by Mark Hayes

Slowly (♩ = ca. 69)

NOT WHILE I'M AROUND

from SWEENEY TODD

Words and Music by
STEPHEN SONDHEIM
Arranged by Mark Hayes

SEASONS OF LOVE
from RENT

Words and Music by
JONATHAN LARSON
Arranged by Mark Hayes

Moderately; with a steady, rhythmic feel (♩ = ca. 92)

SEND IN THE CLOWNS
from the Musical A LITTLE NIGHT MUSIC

Words and Music by
STEPHEN SONDHEIM
Arranged by Mark Hayes

TILL THERE WAS YOU
from Meredith Willson's THE MUSIC MAN

By MEREDITH WILLSON
Arranged by Mark Hayes

Moderately (♩ = ca. 76)

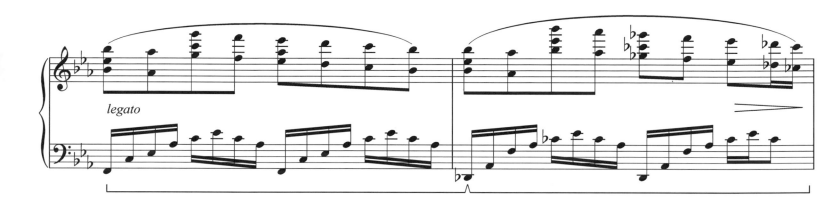

Steady Ballad tempo (♩ = ca. 72)

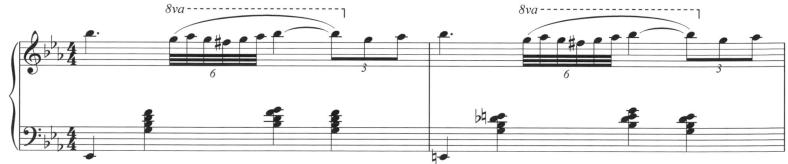